MACHINES RULE!

ON THE FARM

Steve Parker

W
FRANKLIN WATTS
LONDON·SYDNEY

Franklin Watts Australia
Level 17/207 Kent Street
Sydney, NSW 2000

Editor: Jeremy Smith
Design: Billin Design Solutions
Art director: Jonathan Hair

Picture credits: Nigel Cattlin/FLPA
Images: 7b, 26b. Nigel Cattlin/Holt
Studios/ Alamy: 23b. Cancan
Cha/Getty Images: 27b. John Deere
and Company: 3, 7c, 9tl, 10c, 11tr,
16, 18c, 23tr. Foto Natura/FLPA
Images: 25b. Wayne Hutchinson/
FLPA Images: 27tl, 27tr. The Image
Bank/Getty Images: 27c. istockphoto:
8, 11tl, 13tl, 14, 15tr, 15b, 20, 21tr,
22. Peter McDiarmid/Getty Images:
12b. Ricky John Molloy/Getty
Images: 12c. Shutterstock: 2, 4-5, 6,
7, 9tr, 9b, 10b, 11b, 13b, 15c, 15tl,
17b, 17t, 18b, 19c, 19tr, 19b, 19tl,
21b, 21tl, 23tl, 23c, 24b, 24c, 25tr,
28-29, 30, 31. Paul A Souders/
Corbis: 13tr. Alex Wong/Getty
Images: 26c.

Dewey number:629.225

ISBN: 978 1 4451 0627 4

Printed in China.

Franklin Watts is a division of
Hachette Children's Books,
an Hachette UK company.
www.hachette.co.uk

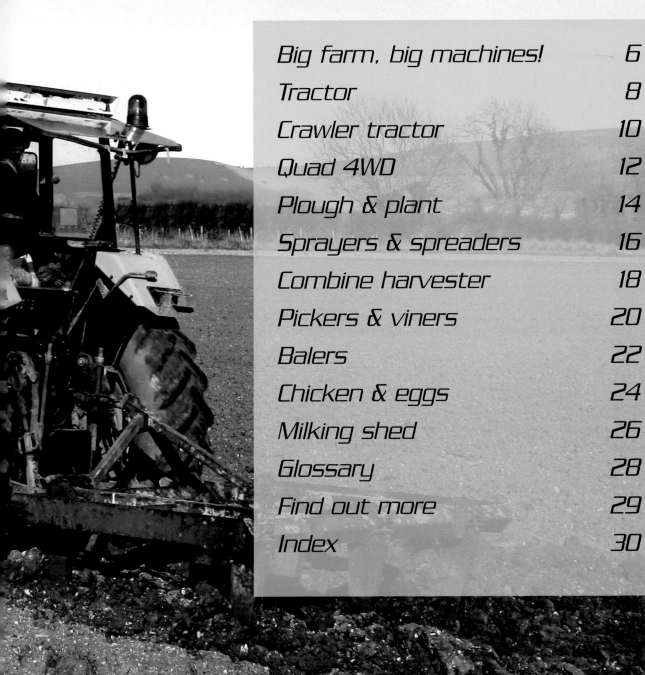

CONTENTS

Big farm, big machines!

In the past, farmers did most jobs by hand, maybe helped by a few horses, oxen or buffalo. Today's farms have massive machinery to take the effort out of most jobs. Many pieces of farm equipment are computer-controlled, with alarms to warn of any problems.

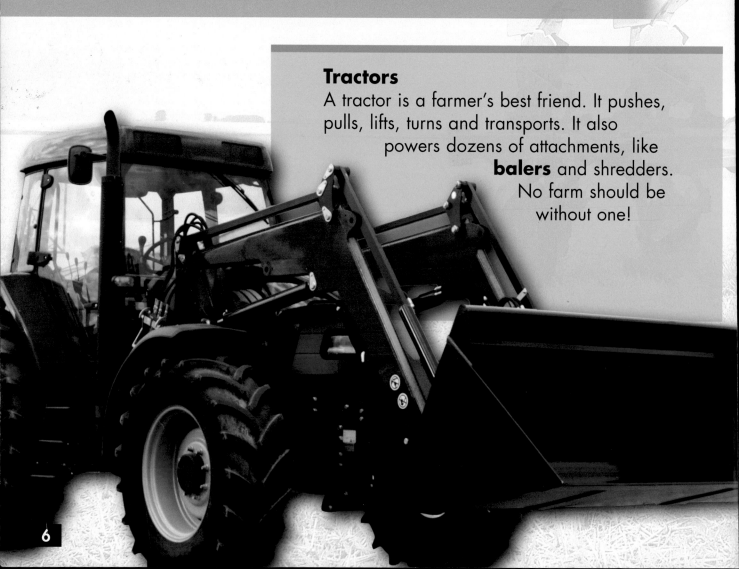

Tractors
A tractor is a farmer's best friend. It pushes, pulls, lifts, turns and transports. It also powers dozens of attachments, like **balers** and shredders. No farm should be without one!

Sprayers and spreaders

When crops have been planted, they need plenty of care. Sprayers and spreaders use chemicals to stop weeds growing and insects destroying crops. They are also used to spray water on crops when there isn't enough rain.

Harvesters and pickers

As crops ripen, harvesters take to the fields. A big combine harvester allows one farmer to do the work of 100 men. But if it goes wrong, it may need an expert to make the machine work properly again!

Looking after livestock

Farmed animals such as cows, sheep, pigs and chickens are called livestock. They need food and water regularly, and somewhere comfortable to live. Many machines are used to help with their care.

Tractor

The farmer's main machine is the tractor. It has many attachments and can do so many jobs, from pulling ploughs and lifting heavy loads to dragging things out of mud – including cars and cows!

Tractors are tough and rugged, with small front wheels for steering, big back wheels for gripping, a powerful diesel engine and bright lights for night work. Sometimes they even get cleaned!

THAT'S INCREDIBLE

In the World Tractor Pulling Championships, tractor drivers compete to see who can pull the heaviest load along a clay track.

Stats and Facts

Extra sets of wheels and tyres stop the tractor sinking into muddy ground.

Tractor attachments include hydraulic lifting arms at the front.

John Deere 7030 series

Maker: John Deere (USA)

Length: 4.8 metres

Width: 2.30 metres

Height: 3.04 metres

Weight: 6 to 7 tonnes

Engine: 6.8 litre six-cylinder diesel

Horsepower: Up to 220

Power take-off: Up to 180 (to drive attachments)

Fuel tank: 390 litres

Top speed: 50 km/h

Crawler tractor

Sometimes even tractors with huge, deep-tread tyres do not have enough power for massive farming jobs. Then it's time to call in the crawler tractor with its tank-like caterpillar tracks.

Some tracks are made of metal or rubber strips linked together.

Some tracked or crawler tractors have one-piece rubber tracks to spread the vehicle's great weight. The tracks' deep ridges grip the ground without causing too much soil damage.

Stats and Facts

On a crawler tractor, each lever in the cabin controls one of the tracks.

MT800B tracked tractor

Maker: Challenger/ AGCO (USA)

Length: 6.75 metres

Width: 3.58 metres

Height: 3.51 metres

Weight: 19 tonnes

Engine: 15.2 litres diesel

Horsepower: Up to 570

Power take-off: Up to 425 (to drive attachments)

Fuel tank: 1,250 litres

Gears: 16 forward, 4 reverse

Top speed: 40 km/h

THAT'S INCREDIBLE

A Challenger tracked tractor planted 572 hectares of seeds in 24 hours. That's the area of a football pitch every two minutes!

Tracked long-reach diggers sometimes come onto farms to do really big tasks. Here, a digger builds a lakeside bank to help stop floods.

Quad 4WD

Years ago, farmers and ranchers and shepherds saddled up their horses to check the fields or round up their animals. Today they climb aboard the farm quad bike (or agri-quad), flick the electric starter, and roar away.

The farm **quad bike** has a powerful motorcycle-type engine and handlebars, tubular steel frame, **4WD** (four wheel drive), **disc brakes**, and sprung swing-arm suspension to smooth out the bumpiest ride

The shepherd still relies on his trusty sheepdog to help round up the flock. But he uses the quad bike almost like a second sheepdog.

Stats and Facts

A quad bike's tyre **tread** has wide-set grooves, which provide plenty of grip but do not get clogged up with mud or soft soil.

Workhorse 360 4X4

Maker: Kawasaki (Japan)

Length: 2.06 metres

Width: 1.20 metres

Height: 1.18 metres

Weight: 274 kilograms

Engine: 362 cc single cylinder 4-stroke

Horsepower: 21

Towing ability: 500 kilograms

Fuel tank: 13.5 litres

Top speed: 65 km/h

THAT'S INCREDIBLE

Expert quad bikers can do amazing stunts and tricks, including wheelies, dirt-drift skids, backflips and complete somersaults!

electrics

air intake

engine

exhaust

Plough & plant

Two of the farm's most important crop machines are the plough, which turns over the soil, and the seed drill, which plants seeds into the prepared soil.

THAT'S INCREDIBLE

In the World Ploughing Championships, each competitor has three hours to plough an area 100 metres by 20 metres. There are points for how straight, neat, even and deep the furrows are.

Stats and Facts

Fields are prepared by ploughs towed by tractors.

Tillers, crumblers and rollers then smooth the field ready for planting.

Megant 600 pneumatic seed drill

Maker: Kuhn (USA)

Transport width: 2.98 metres

Working drill width: 6 metres

Number of seed rows: 40

Row spacing: 15 cm

Hopper volume: 1,850 litres

Hopper height: 2.1 metres

Working speed: 8–15 km/h

Features: Cross-board levelling bar, non-protruding side markers

A seed **drill** holds seeds. As the tractor goes along, the drill pushes seeds into the soil.

Sprayers & spreaders

A crop sprayer holds chemicals and water in the central tank.

The trailer sprayer folds up its boom arms to travel along roads and lanes.

Once seeds are planted, there's still plenty of work to do. Sprayers apply water containing fertilisers to feed the plants, and chemical pesticides to get rid of insects, weeds and moulds. Spreaders apply these as powders or pellets.

Planes, such as this Chipmunk, and helicopters can crop-spray faster than tractors. But these flying machines are expensive. Most farmers hire them and their pilots by the day.

Chipmunk crop-spraying ultralight aircraft

Maker: RAF (UK)

Length: 7.75 metres

Wingspan: 10.47 metres

Take-off run: 205 metres

Empty weight: 646 kg

Horsepower: 145

Fuel tank: 70 litres

Sprayer tank: 160 litres

Top speed: 222 km/h

Spray area: 124 hectares per hour

THAT'S INCREDIBLE

Some crop sprayers have booms that open out in sections, to a width of more than 50 metres – twice the length of a tennis court!

In dry weather, massive irrigators several kilometres long spray water onto crops. They crawl along very slowly, their wheels turned by fan-like blades inside, spun by the water pressure.

Combine harvester

The biggest machine on most farms is the combine harvester or 'combine'. It brings together (combines) several harvesting jobs that used to be done by separate machines.

Most combines have their own powerful diesel engine that works all the machinery on board. The crop, such as wheat, barley or rye, is cut (reaped).

The on-board **satnav** tells the farmer where to cut first.

A rotating reel pulls the crop against a low blade, which slices the crop stem.

CR9080 combine harvester

Maker: New Holland (Italy)

Length: Approx 6 metres

Width: 3.5 metres without cutters

Height: 3.96 metres

Weight: 15.4 tonnes

Engine: Iveco Cursor 10 diesel fuel-injection

Horsepower: Up to 458

Cutting width: Up to 9.5 metres

Grain tank: 10,500 litres

Grain unloading speed: 110 litres per second

Lighting: 17 floods and spots for night work

The grain is stored in the on-board tank, while the straw (stems) can be chopped up and blow into the trailer.

THAT'S INCREDIBLE

The world record for combine harvesting is more than 200 hectares in 24 hours. That's the area of one football pitch every six minutes.

Pickers & viners

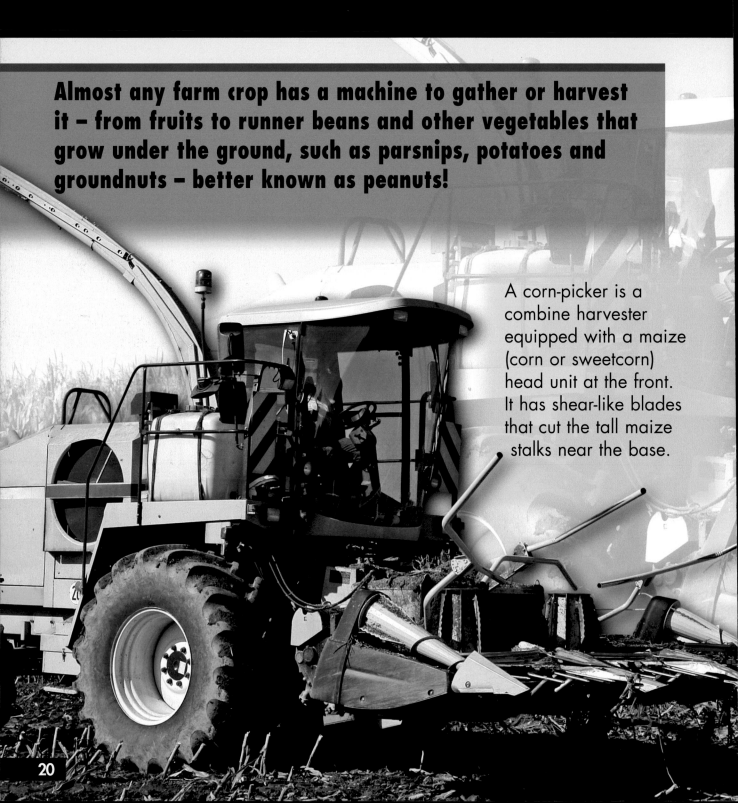

Almost any farm crop has a machine to gather or harvest it – from fruits to runner beans and other vegetables that grow under the ground, such as parsnips, potatoes and groundnuts – better known as peanuts!

A corn-picker is a combine harvester equipped with a maize (corn or sweetcorn) head unit at the front. It has shear-like blades that cut the tall maize stalks near the base.

Grapes are grown not just to eat, but to make into wine and juices. The 'over-the-row' harvester shakes or vibrates the grape bunches from the vines, all without damaging the grapes.

Nairn 1230 grape harvester

Maker: Nairn (New Zealand)

Length: 5.6 metres

Width: 3.5 metres

Height: 4 metres

Weight 7.5 tonnes

Engine: Cummins 125 HP 4-cylinder turbo-diesel

Minimum picking height: 0.5 metres

Picking chamber width: 0.8 metres plus

Tunnel height: 2.03 metres

Road speed: 30 km/h

THAT'S INCREDIBLE

Garden peas are ripest and sweetest for just 12 hours. They are tested for sugar and tenderness, harvested and frozen, all within 2 1/2 hours.

Potato harvesters 'lift' (dig up) the crop and shake the soil from them.

Balers

Crops like wheat and rice are grown for their seeds or grains. But other parts of the plants can come in very useful too. Often they are squeezed and tied into bales.

THAT'S INCREDIBLE
In some parts of the world, people use hay to make barns and even houses to live in!

Stats and Facts

Some balers are towed by tractors. Others are **self-propelled**.

Hay bales are the long dried stalks of grasses and similar plants. Farmers feed hay to all kinds of farm animals, especially in the winter.

5410 Rebel Baler for round bales

Type: Tractor towed

Maker: Vermeer (USA)

Length: 3.91 metres

Width: 2.41 metres

Height: 2.62 metres

Weight: 2.1 tonnes

Power needed: 50 horsepower

Bale diameter: 1.52 metres

Bale length: 1.2 metres

Bale weight: Up to 450 kilograms depending on crop

Netwrap time: Less than 10 seconds per bale

Some bales are wrapped in plastic to keep in their moisture.

Chicken & eggs

There are more than 30 billion chickens in the world – five for every person! They are reared mainly for their eggs and meat. Many machines help farmers give their flocks constant care, 24 hours every day.

Chicken eggs take three weeks to hatch. **Incubators** keep them warm at 37° C, and rollers slowly turn the eggs so they are heated evenly.

Stats and Facts

Once hatched, the fluffy chicks are kept warm and dry. They grow quickly when fed on special food. They will become either laying hens, or chickens raised for meat, called broilers and roasters.

Hatchmaster A Incubator

Maker: Brinsea (USA)

Type: Still Air tabletop egg incubator

Length: 81 centimetres

Width: 60 centimetres

Height: 25 centimetres

Weight: 11 kilograms

Capacity: 256 quail eggs, 176 pheasant eggs, 104 hen eggs, 91 duck eggs, 50 goose eggs

Egg turning: Automatic

Power consumption: 55 watts average, 115 watts maximum

THAT'S INCREDIBLE

There are almost 200 varieties of chicken. Champion laying hens produce more than 300 eggs each year.

Machines fill food and water dishes regularly for the growing chicks.

Milking shed

Milk is a tasty drink that is good for your health, especially for growing children. Milk is collected from cows using all kinds of different kinds of machinery and equipment.

THAT'S INCREDIBLE
Most milk comes from cows. Around the world , however, people also milk goats, sheep, camels, water buffalo, horses, yaks and reindeer!

Cows are usually milked twice each day, early morning and evening. Here, cows wait to go into the milking shed.

In this rotary milking shed, the cows munch food as they go around on a turntable.

AutoRotor Magnum 40

Maker: WestfaliaSurge (Germany)

Design: Rotary milking parlour

Platform: Poured concrete

Roller bearings: Nylon

Stalls: Up to 48

Cows milked per hour: 100 or more

Angle of stalls: 40°

Operator: Within circle

Milk meter: Metatron digital, with DairyPlan computer software

This farm worker puts the suction nozzles or teat-cups onto the cow's teats. The milk is sucked along pipes into a big tank.

Milk can be heat-treated, or **pasteurised**, to kill germs and stop it going sour. Some milk is put into cartons and bottles. Milk is also used to make cheeses, creams, yogurts and other dairy foods, including ice cream!

27

Glossary

4WD
Four wheel drive, where the engine turns all four roadwheels rather than just the front two or rear two.

Baler
A machine that gathers plants such as hay, straw or herbs, presses them into big brick shapes and ties them with twine (string).

Caterpillar track
A 'crawler' or long ridged belt in a loop shape that goes round and round, with wheels inside it, as used on tanks, construction vehicles and big tractors.

Disc brakes
Brakes that work when two pads, fixed to the vehicle, press on a ring-shaped disc that rotates with the roadwheel.

Drill
In farming, a machine that pushes seeds into the soil to plant them.

Hydraulic
Working by the force of a high-pressure liquid, usually water or a special oil.

Incubator
A container that keeps things warm, from chicken eggs and baby plants to human babies.

Pasteurise
To kill germs in liquids or foods by heating them.

Pesticide
A chemical that kills animal pests such as insects, mites and some types of worm.

Quad bike
A combination of motorcycle and car, with four wheels but no enclosed bodywork.

Satnav
Satellite navigation, finding the way using signals from GPS (Global Positioning System) satellites high in space.

Self-propelled
A vehicle or machine with its own motor or engine, so that it can move along under its own power.

Tread
On a tyre, the surface pattern of grooves and bumps which grip the ground.

Find out more

Websites

http://www.kidcyber.com.au/topics/farms.htm
A large, wide-ranging site on farms and farm animals.

http://www.lackhamfarm.co.uk/about/machinery.asp
Pictures and details of vehicles and machinery at Lackham Farm and Estate, an educational and training site for Wiltshire College in western England.

http://science.howstuffworks.com/inside-tractor.htm
About tractors, especially tractor pulls and similar competitions.

http://www.ploughmen.co.uk/british.htm
The skills of ploughing and the annual British National Ploughing Championships.

http://onthefarm.e2bn.org
Life and times on the farm from E2BN, the government-established broadband learning network for the East of England.

http://www.hse.gov.uk/agriculture/pdf/childsafetyce.pdf
British government site about the dangers of farming and how to stay safe.

Books

Tractors (Big Machines), by David and Penny Glover, Franklin Watts, 2007

Tractors (On the Go), by David and Penny Glover, Wayland, 2007

Tractors (Mega Machine Drivers), by Chris Oxlade, Franklin Watts, 2009

Tractors (Working Wheels), by Annabel Savery, Franklin Watts, 2009

Note to parents and teachers:
Every effort has been made by the Publishers to ensure that the websites in this book are suitable for children, that they are of the highest educational value, and that they contain no inappropriate or offensive material. However, because of the nature of the Internet, it is impossible to guarantee that the contents of these sites will not be altered. We strongly advise that Internet access is supervised by a responsible adult.

Index